NATURAL KITCHEN

First published in 2010 by Blue Sky Books Ltd
2nd Floor, Berkeley Square House, Berkeley Square, London W1J 6BD
www.blueskybooks.co.uk

British Cataloguing-in-Publication Data:
A catalogue record of this book is available from the British Library.

ISBN 978-1-907309-05-2

Designed by Spirit Design Consultants, London
www.spirit-design.com

Printed and bound in China through Printworks Int. Ltd.

Contents

INTRODUCTION

The kitchen is the heart of the home and
the hub of the house.

The Natural Kitchen shows us simple and effective
ways to create a kitchen that is relaxed and informal.
With practical hints on keeping things clean and
tidy, the organic way, through to looking
after kitchen tools and appliances.

And, very much at the centre of kitchen life is food.
Timeless cook's advice blends with the modern, from
storing and preserving fruit, through to tending a herb
garden. The natural kitchen is above all a working
kitchen, where the pretty is also practical. Decorative
appliances and inspirational accessories combine
to create attractive displays and essential storage.

This simple book celebrates the place
we cook, eat and get together.

THE NATURAL KITCHEN

The kitchen is the most used room in the house and works well when it has a relaxed, informal feel to it. Neutral, simple colours are perfect. They not only create a sense of calm, but also make the choice of accessories and furnishings much easier.

✳

A neutral colour scheme means you can change the kitchen's look easily with soft-patterned curtains and matching tablecloths. Crockery and glassware can also be updated regularly to refresh the look.

✳

With its comfortable, relaxed feel, wood is the perfect choice for the natural kitchen. A wooden dresser is ideal for displaying favourite accessories and tableware. The unique textures and tones of wood help it to blend beautifully with a variety of materials.

✳

An assortment of chairs gives a kitchen a unique rustic
feel and is perfect for mixing together various colours
and fabric designs. If you can't quite decide which fabric
to chose, combining several co-ordinating patterns
may be the option.

❋

A solid, wooden kitchen table not only looks
attractive, it also serves as a versatile work surface.
It can be left bare for an attractive natural look
or covered with pretty crisp linen. A plain white
tablecloth and napkins is also a simple and inviting look.

❋

Old buckets filled with dried cow parsley give
an earthy, lived-in feel. Salvage yards and flea
markets are perfect for picking up unusual
items such as cast iron buckets, wrought iron
accessories and interesting kitchen equipment.

❋

To update the look of cupboards with glass doors,
attach an attractive wallpaper design inside the doors.
Choose a pattern that blends with the style
and colour of the wood.

A natural kitchen makes the most of any daylight by
keeping windows dressed simply with light neutral
curtain fabrics and unfussy blinds. Simple rattan and
effortless roman blinds in off-white and ivory are
perfect for maximising natural light.

Wooden and wrought iron curtain poles are ideal to
finish the look. Keep the accessories simple or contrast
a decorative finish with a plain, natural fabric.

Don't underestimate the positive effect of fresh linen.
Crisp tea towels and neatly ironed tablecloths
are instantly uplifting and welcoming.

�֎

Matching oven gloves, pretty aprons and decorative
ironing board covers are simple ways to co-ordinate
and add a touch of colour to the kitchen.

✖

It's the simple touches that create a natural, easy,
yet stylish feel to a kitchen. A simple glass tumbler
filled with daisies or a selection of dried herbs can
both be displayed effortlessly for visual impact.

✖

COOK'S TOOLS

Good pans are an essential part of a smooth
running kitchen. It is well worth investing in good
quality, solid pans and caring for them well
to get the most out of them.

✳

Always fill pans with hot water as soon as you
empty them. If the pans are particularly soiled
add a solution of hot water and washing soda.
Cold water is best for pans used to cook
porridge, potatoes and rice.

✳

A trolley or butcher's block are both perfect for adding
a little extra space in the kitchen. They can be used
for preparing food, hanging kitchen utensils, or
standing hot pans. The drawers are particularly useful
for storing small gadgets and kitchen knives.

✳

Two chopping boards are ideal, one for vegetables
and one for meat. When chopping raw meat,
always scrub the board well after use.

✳

Wooden chopping boards are best cared for by regular
scrubbing with a stiff-bristled brush and hot water,
to remove any stains. The occasional wipe with a little
vegetable oil will protect it from splitting and
warping and keep it in good condition.

✳

To clear any food odours, rub the board with half
a lemon dipped in coarse salt. Salt is a natural
disinfectant. Your chopping board is best
stored where plenty of air can circulate.

✳

Salad bowls are best not washed, unless really necessary.
Instead wipe the bowl with kitchen towel and rub
in a little vegetable oil to keep it in good condition.

✺

Always use wooden or plastic salad servers,
not metal ones. Metal can bruise lettuce leaves
and also taint the edges.

✺

A good knife is essential to every kitchen.
Sharpening stones are the best option to keep
knives in pristine condition. Hot water can warp
blades, so knives are best washed by hand in cold
or lukewarm water. Make sure they are dried
thoroughly. For extra protection, store in
a wooden knife block.

✺

CLEAN AND SIMPLE

Natural and organic cleaning solutions are a safe, simple and popular alternative to chemical cleaners. Most of the ingredients you need are readily available in your kitchen cupboard.

❋

For a mild, gentle cleaner mix 2 heaped tablespoons of bicarbonate of soda with 1 tablespoon of white vinegar. Store the cleaner in an airtight container. This can be used for everyday cleaning of work surfaces and woodwork.

❋

Clean all coffee making equipment such as grinders, expresso machines and perculators regularly. Coffee beans produce a particular oil which if allowed to build up can make the coffee taste bitter.

❋

For sparkling crystal, rinse in a weak solution of
water and vinegar

Wash stained flower vases with 1 tablespoon vinegar
and 1 tablespoon salt in warm water. Allow the water to
stand for several hours in the vase, shaking occasionally.

Venetian blinds can be cleaned by soaking a pair
of fabric gloves in soapy water. Squeeze any excess
water out of the gloves, put them on and slide a finger
carefully along each slat of the blind to remove any dust.

Kitchen sponges and cloths can be easily freshened. Mix a handful of salt, 1 tablespoon of washing soda and 4 cups of warm water in a bowl. Place the cloths in the solution, leave for a couple of minutes then rinse in cold water. Allow the cloths to dry.

To keep the kitchen pipe work running freely pour a cup of washing soda down the sink and then follow with 1 cup of white vinegar. Leave this without rinsing for 15 minutes, then pour down a kettle full of boiling water.

Regularly pouring boiling water down the kitchen sink will melt away any grease and keep the pipes clean. Adding a few drops of vanilla essence will create a pleasant odour.

Stains on tiles can be gently removed by rubbing
on salt with half a lemon.

✾

Shine slate the natural way, by wiping with a few drops
of lemon and gently polishing with a soft, dry cloth.

✾

Care for granite work surfaces by wiping regularly
and thoroughly with a hot cloth.

✾

Try rubbing in crushed salt with a dish cloth
to remove tea stains from china cups.

✾

Keep chrome taps shining by polishing them regularly
with a cloth soaked in white vinegar.

✾

Always use a wax free polish when polishing
kitchen cabinets and tables. Wax locks grease stains
and moisture into wood, softening its surface.

※

For sealed wood surfaces, place pots and pans
on a tile or pan holder to prevent any burns
or scorches to the wood's surface.

※

To treat unsealed wood, rub the wood with boiled
linseed oil, wiping off any excess with a soft cloth.
For scorch marks and stains, try rubbing on salt and lemon.

※

THE HEALTHY KITCHEN

There are a number of easy, yet effective ways
to keep an organic, healthy kitchen. A few simple
actions, that are easy to implement, but
have definite results.

✸

Keeping the kitchen well ventilated makes it a much
healthier place to be. Managing moisture in the
kitchen also has a positive effect on the whole home.
Keep the door closed when cooking to reduce
the escape of steam and vapour that can lead
to mould and mildew.

✸

Keep a recycling corner. Any biodegradable items
can be put into a mini kitchen bin and then taken out
when necessary to the compost heap. Recycling can
be attractive. Use interesting containers such as lined
wicker baskets and cast iron buckets, keeping it
practical and attractive.

✸

Invest in good quality cookware and utensils
that will stand the test of time, rather than items that
need replacing frequently. Cast iron is a good choice.
It is sturdy, easy to look after and looks attractive.

Install a home water filter. They look stylish,
are easy to install and supply freshly filtered water
at the turn of a tap.

Avoid corrosive cleaners such as bleach on sinks,
as they can scratch the steel. Organic solutions are
a more gentle option and also more hygienic.

Shopping

Milk   Olive Oil
Honey   Brown Suger
Bread

Place the fridge in a cool spot, not next to the oven
or in the sun. Ensure there is good circulation around
the coils and keep them dusted regularly. The door
seals should be kept clean and in good working order.
Ensure the fridge is regularly defrosted
for maximum efficiency.

To keep the fridge smelling naturally fresh, wipe
over the inside with a mixture of vanilla and water.

Lemon is also perfect for washing and keeping the
fridge, bin or kitchen compost container fresh.
Mix a solution of I teaspoon lemon juice to 4 cups
water for natural freshness. Fill a spray bottle with
the solution and use as necessary.

PRETTY AND PRACTICAL

Rails and rods are ideal for hanging regularly used
kitchen equipment. Butcher's hooks are perfect
for spoons, spatulas and whisks, they'll be easy
to reach and look attractive on display.

✳

Kitchen appliances can act as a focal point in
the kitchen, creating a distinctive and individual
look. Appliances have become statement pieces
in their own right, with old fashioned refrigerators,
retro style food mixers and character rich, butlers'
sinks adding old-fashioned flair to the kitchen.
Combining old and new compliments
the natural kitchen perfectly.

✳

Other classic pieces of equipment such as designer
juice squeezers, coffee percolators and stylish
espresso machines are both fashionable and practical.
Appliances with interesting shapes, lines and quality
finishes can complete a look, providing the perfect
way of combining beauty and utility.

✳

Tableware and cooking items are wonderful
for creating a decorative, lived in look. Try mixing
and matching simple crockery with a few favourite
porcelain pieces. Old fashioned storage jars, a few
carefully selected vintage tea caddies and enamel
flour bins work together to create a simple yet
stylish look. The result is pretty and practical.

As well as creating a distinctive, individual look,
displays of favourite tableware and ceramics can
be updated or added to regularly. Refreshing the
look is simple and easy. This mix and match approach
to displaying china, cutlery and glassware gives
a relaxed feel to the kitchen and helps you build
a kitchen with its own style, which
can be updated seasonally.

A simple, white-painted display cabinet is perfect
for showcasing any accessories collection. Even fine
china looks down to earth on a simple unit or shelf.

Pots and pans are perfect for a kitchen display.
Stacks of cast iron and copper pans are interesting,
eye-catching and look very much at home against
a neutral coloured wall. They also look good
stacked on a plain, unfussy shelf or dresser.

Woven metal baskets are perfect for displaying
fruit. The fruit can be seen and more importantly
breathe. Fresh fruit is colourful and can be constantly
updated as fruit is eaten and new fruit added.

NEAT AND TIDY

Glass containers are excellent for display and storage,
as they can be filled with interesting food items,
such as earthy coloured spices, wonderful pasta shapes,
exotic tea collections and colourful home made jams.

✳

Earthenware storage jars add a solid, practical feel
to the kitchen and look wonderful crammed with spatulas,
wooden spoons, whisks and other kitchen utensils.

✳

Plate racks are a versatile addition to the kitchen.
Fit them inside a cupboard or display them on the wall
over a frequently used work surface. They are practical,
as flat tableware can be slotted away and left to dry.
They also add to the decor and are perfect
for displaying favourite pieces.

✳

Keep cupboards neat, tidy and organised by having a good clear out once every season. Get rid of any foods past their sell by date and any items you never use. Update your food cupboards with delicious seasonal ingredients.

Designate a kitchen drawer for handy items such as string, selotape, scissors and similar items, that way they'll always be in one place and you can find them quickly and easily.

Use a key holder or a combination of decorative hooks, so keys are easy to find when you're in a hurry. Attaching clear labels will make them easily identifiable and stop them getting mislaid.

Invest in a stylish recycling holder for paper, or use a favourite wicker basket or patterned storage box. This will help you keep on top of junk mail.

A pin board is ideal for shopping lists or simple reminder messages. It can be decorated with favourite postcards, photographs or dried flowers and herbs. Keep a shopping list pad nearby too, so you can copy down any must-buy items.

A set of handy hooks is useful for frequently used items such as shopping bags, umbrellas and dog leads.

FRESH FOOD

A small kitchen garden is a wonderful addition
to the natural kitchen and can provide an abundant
supply of fresh herbs and salad vegetables.

※

Easy to grow vegetables include peppers, carrots,
cucumbers, lettuce, garlic, peas, onions, squash, radish,
tomatoes, beans and beetroot.

※

Herbs are a lovely feature growing in a window
box or a row of terracotta pots. Popular herbs
suitable for pots are chives, mint, basil and bergamot.
Most herbs are best grown in full sunlight and
free-draining soil and best gathered as they
come into flower, as this is when their
flavour is strongest.

※

To freeze herbs, collect the shoots when they're
young and tender. Wash them thoroughly in cold
water and cut the herbs into small sections. Place
them in the compartments of an ice cube tray
and fill with water and freeze immediately.
The best herbs for freezing are parsley,
chives, basil and borage.

※

Rosemary is renowned for its affinity with lamb,
dill is perfect with fish and parsley makes a good
all round garnish. More unusual combinations
are ginger mint with tomatoes and apple mint
as a delicious alternative in mint sauce.

※

To firm up soft, over ripe tomatoes, place them in the fridge
in a bowl of salted water. Leave for about an hour.

※

To skin a clove of garlic, pound it with the side of a heavy knife and the skin will slip off easily.

Limp celery can be freshened up by wrapping it in newspaper, then standing the celery upright in a jug of cold water.

Rinse away any frost on frozen vegetables before boiling. They will cook quicker and retain more of their taste.

To soften the skins of new potatoes so they peel easier, soak them in water with a tablespoonful of salt.

Grating oranges and lemons is much easier
if they're frozen. It's best to put them in the freezer
an hour or two before you need them.

※

Allow home-made jam to cool and thicken a little
before you put it into jars. This stops the fruit
from sinking to the bottom.

※

To store strawberries in the refrigerator
before eating, put them in a sieve or colander
to allow the air to circulate around them.

※

Don't store bananas in the fridge or next to other fruit,
they will ripen too quickly and blacken other fruit.

※

Items like paprika, red peppers, cayenne and chilli
should be stored in a dark, cool place, as they
are easily affected by heat and humidity.

❋

Olive oil can be kept longer if you add a pinch
of sugar to the bottle then put it in the refrigerator.

❋

To keep rice white, add a few drops
of lemon to the water when cooking.

❋

To crisp a loaf of bread, hold the loaf very briefly
under a running cold tap and give it a good shake.
Place it in a hot oven for about 10 minutes.
It will come out as soft and crusty as freshly baked.

❋

To eliminate the smell of onions from your hands
rub with celery or parsley.

�֍

To prevent cooking aromas from lingering, place
a small bowl of white vinegar next to the oven
while cooking, it even works on strong
odours such as fried fish.

✖

To remove fruit stains from your hands, mix
a little caster sugar and olive oil into a paste.
Rub the paste well into the skin, leave for a few
minutes then wash your hands in warm soapy
water. If the stains are particularly
stubborn, repeat again.

✖

PHOTOGRAPHY CREDITS